DORLING KINDERSLEY *READERS*

Level 2

Dinosaur Dinners
Fire Fighter!
Bugs! Bugs! Bugs!
Slinky, Scaly Snakes!
Animal Hospital
The Little Ballerina
Munching, Crunching, Sniffing
   and Snooping
The Secret Life of Trees
Winking, Blinking, Wiggling
   and Waggling

Astronaut: Living in Space
Twisters!
Holiday! Celebration Days
   around the World
The Story of Pocahontas
Horse Show
Survivors: The Night the Titanic Sank
Eruption! The Story of Volcanoes
The story of Columbus
LEGO: Castle Under Attack!
LEGO: Rocket Rescue

Level 3

Spacebusters
Beastly Tales
Shark Attack!
Titanic
Invaders from Outer Space
Movie Magic
Plants Bite Back!
Time Traveler
Bermuda Triangle
Tiger Tales
Aladdin
Heidi
Zeppelin: The Age of the Airship
Spies

Terror on the Amazon
Disasters at Sea
The Story of Anne Frank
Abraham Lincoln: Lawyer, Leader,
   Legend
George Washington: Soldier, Hero,
   President
Extreme Sports
LEGO: Mission to the Arctic
NFL: Troy Aikman
NFL: Super Bowl Heroes
NFL: Peyton Manning
MLB: Home Run Heroes
MLB: Roberto Clemente

Level 4

Days of the Knights
Volcanoes
Secrets of the Mummies
Pirates!
Horse Heroes
Trojan Horse
Micromonsters
Going for Gold!
Extreme Machines
Flying Ace: The Story of Amelia Earhart
Robin Hood
Black Beauty
Free at Last! The Story of
   Martin Luther King, Jr.
Joan of Arc
Spooky Spinechillers
Welcome to The Globe! The
   Story of Shakespeare's Theater
Antarctic Adventure
Space Station

Atlantis
Dinosaur Detectives
Danger on the Mountain: Scaling
   the World's Highest Peaks
Crime Busters
LEGO: Race for Survival
NFL: NFL's Greatest Upsets
NFL: Terrell Davis
NFL: Rambling Running Backs
WCW: Going for Goldberg
WCW: Feel the Sting!
WCW: Fit for the Title
WCW: Finishing Moves
MLB: Strikeout Kings
MLB: Super Shortstops: Jeter,
   Nomar, and A-Rod
The Story of the X-Men: How it
   all Began
Creating the X-Men: How Comic
   Books Come to Life

A Note to Parents

Dorling Kindersley Readers is a compelling program for beginning readers, designed in conjunction with leading literacy experts, including Dr. Linda Gambrell, Director of the School of Education at Clemson University. Dr. Gambrell has served on the Board of Directors of the International Reading Association and as President of the National Reading Conference.

Beautiful illustrations and superb full-color photographs combine with engaging, easy-to-read stories to offer a fresh approach to each subject in the series. Each Dorling Kindersley Reader is guaranteed to capture a child's interest while developing his or her reading skills, general knowledge, and love of reading.

The four levels of Dorling Kindersley Readers are aimed at different reading abilities, enabling you to choose the books that are exactly right for your child:

Level 1 – Beginning to read
Level 2 – Beginning to read alone
Level 3 – Reading alone
Level 4 – Proficient readers

The "normal" age at which a child begins to read can be anywhere from three to eight years old, so these levels are intended only a general guideline.

No matter which level you select, you can be sure that you are helpingyour child learn to read,then read to learn!

Dorling **DK** Kindersley

LONDON, NEW YORK, SYDNEY, DELHI, PARIS,
MUNICH, and JOHANNESBURG

Project Editor Esther Ripley
Art Editor Jane Horne
Senior Art Editor Clare Shedden
Series Editor Deborah Lock
US Editor Regina Kahney
Production Shivani Pandey
Picture Researcher Sean Hunter
Jacket Designer
Sophia Tampakopoulos
Indexer Christine Headley

Reading Consultant
Linda B. Gambrell, Ph.D

Extreme Sports Consultants
Tony Hansen, Steve Glidewell,
Chris Anthony, Jason Bell

First American Edition, 2001
00 01 02 03 04 05 10 9 8 7 6 5 4 3 2 1
Published in the United States by DK Publishing, Inc.
95 Madison Avenue, New York, New York 10016

Published in Great Britain by Dorling Kindersley Limited.

A Cataloging-in-Publication record is available
from the Library of Congress.
ISBN 0-7894-7883-8 (plc) 0-7894-7884-6 (pb)

Color reproduction by Colourscan, Singapore
Printed and bound in China by L Rex Printing Co., Ltd.

The publisher would like to thank the following for their kind
permission to reproduce their photographs:
a=above; c=center; b=below; l=left; r=right; t=top;
Allsport: Agence Vandystadt - Didier Klein 46br; Darren England 33br; Mike
Hewitt 47tl; Harry How 46bl; Jamie Squire 47tc; **Jason Bell:** 38c, 39bcl, 40br, 41,
42cl, 43tr, 43, 44, 45br; **Corbis:** AFP 39bl; Duomo 5tr, 15br; Richard Hamilton
Smith 16bl; Craig Lovell 23br; Galen Rowell 25br; TempSport - Jerome Prevost 47br;
Patrick Ward 17t; Karl Weatherly 22; **Empics Ltd:** Steve Etherington 46tr, 49br; Jed
Leicester 47tr; **Jack Gescheidt:** 2br, 14b, 14t, 15tr, 18-19, 20; **Courtesy of K2
Skates:** 16tr; Kent A. Kantowski: 23t, 24, 27, 28t, 29b; **Popperfoto:** Wolfgang
Luif/Reuters 39tr; Thomas Ulrich/Reuters 39br; **RPM Photographic:** 4b, 6br, 7tr, 7b,
8tl, 9, 10tl, 10-11b, 12b, 13t; **RPM** 3bc; **Science Photo Library;** Scott Camazine
37br; Photographs Courtesy of PACE Motor Sports, Inc., n/k/a SFX Motor Sports
Group, a company of SFX Entertainment, Inc., a subsidiary of Clear Channel
Communications, Inc.: 30b, 31tr, 32tl, 33, 34, 35tr, 35br, 36t, 37tr; **Sporting
Pictures (UK) Ltd:** D. Blane 39bcr; **Unity Magazine:** Steve Glidewell 46bc.

Jacket: **gettyone.stone:** front; **Sporting Pictures (UK) Ltd:** back tl.

see our complete
catalog at
www.dk.com

Contents

DORLING KINDERSLEY *READERS*

READING
3
ALONE

EXTREME
SPORTS

Written by Richard Platt

A Dorling Kindersley Book

Living close to the edge

Extreme sports are all about seeking thrills, taking risks, and staying alive. Many of them are played in dangerous places. Steep skiers and snowboarders seek out the highest mountain slopes. Base jumpers, hang gliders, and sky surfers pitch themselves into thin air. Whitewater rafters look for the fastest, roughest routes downriver.

Some extreme sports are a showcase for great tricks. Inline skaters and skateboarders learned their skills on city sidewalks – now huge audiences watch their gravity-defying stunts.

Extreme sports competitors need top-of-the-line equipment – wheels, skis, parachutes, rafts, and engine power. Then they use gravity, muscle, wind, and sheer nerve to go faster, jump higher, or fall farther.

The stories that follow are about five exciting sports. Each story describes a contest or a place where extreme sports enthusiasts test their skills to the limit.

Whitewater rafting

The red truck rattled to a halt and six eager rafters tumbled out onto the track. Below them, the Río Futaleufú (Fu-ta-lay-oo-FOO) wound like a long turquoise snake through the snow-topped mountains of Chile.

As the River Raiders unloaded their raft, everyone talked about the race.

"Futaleufú means Big River," said Dan. "After we reach Inferno Canyon, it's class-five rapids all the way."

"Wait till we hit the Terminator," said Rob. "That rapid goes on forever."

Numbering of rapids
Rapids are numbered to show how fast and difficult they are. Class-five rapids are for experts only – spectacular and dangerous.

Playing safe
Rafters wear high-flotation
jackets and helmets in case
they are swept onto rocks.
In cold water, they wear
heat-retaining rubber suits.

The parking lot soon became a
tangle of paddles and ropes. It took
nearly an hour before the first group
of five crews climbed aboard their rafts
and paddled downriver to the start.

"Five, four, three, two, one, GO!" The River Raiders paddled furiously, but another raft swept ahead of them.

"The Tiger Rafters," muttered Dan through gritted teeth. "They won last year."

All five rafts shot through the first rapid, but the next was much harder.

The Tigers' raft rode the first wave, its front lifting clear of the water. When it crashed down again, the crew vanished in a cloud of spray. Then it was the River Raiders' turn to ride the roller-coaster of water. They braced themselves for the shock.

The river bubbled and boiled beneath the air-filled raft. The raft bounced, twisted, and shook, and the crew was soaked with spray. But an instant later the water was calm. It was as if the river had flown into a rage, and then regained its temper almost as quickly.

As they rounded a bend in the river, Dan shouted, "We're catching up!" The two rafts were neck and neck as they plunged into the Terminator.

Suddenly, the Raiders were on their own. The Tiger Rafters' raft had flipped, and the crew was bobbing in the water.

Dan looked back and let out a whoop of joy – just in time to see a pair of legs disappearing over the side. A big wave had knocked Rob overboard and was sweeping him toward the riverbank.

"Rob's gone in!" Dan shouted.

"He's okay – but we'll lose points at the finish if we go on without him."

The crew paddled across river and struggled to keep the raft steady as Rob lunged for the side. Two rafts swept past before he was able to haul himself in.

At the finish line, the exhausted crew hauled their raft out of the water. They had come in third.

"Yeah, but the Tiger Rafters aren't even home yet," said Dan. "And next year, the Whitewater Challenge Cup is definitely going to the Raiders." ❖

Aggressive inline skating

"Mick pulled some awesome tricks. His alley-oop fishbrain on the coping was sooo cool!"

"And did you catch that backside royale? That was really great!"

As usual, the top of the vert ramp at the San Francisco X Games was buzzing with skate talk.

Mel, one of only four girls in the aggressive inline skating trials, tried not to listen. She just wanted a high enough score to get into the finals.

She had to concentrate on her run. The vert ramp below her was one of the biggest she had skated on. It was fast enough for her to pull off some neat tricks – but so steep she could easily end up flat on her face.

Vert ramps
Vert skaters perform on half-pipes – U-shaped ramps over ten feet tall. Skaters win points for style, difficulty, and "big airs" – tricks high in the air.

Aggressive inline skates
Ankle-hugging cuffs give extra control. "Grind plates" between the wheels prevent damage when skaters slide down rails and kerbs.

Mel fiddled nervously with her skates. They were top-of-the-line aggressive inline skates, the best she had ever owned. She thought back to her first pair – they had been fine for gliding

smoothly along the sidewalks. But when she began to watch the inline skaters in her neighborhood, she realized there was much more to skating than flat pavements.

As soon as she started doing jumps and grinds – speeding down curbs and rails on the gap between the wheels – her skates just fell apart. She had taken many falls learning the simplest tricks. Mel stroked the scar on her knee – that cut had needed three stitches.

"Hey, Mel! You're up next," shouted the steward. Mel pulled on her helmet, took a deep breath at the lip of the ramp, and then dropped in.

On a vert ramp, skaters perform grinds on the coping – a rail that runs along the top of the ramp.

She sped smoothly down the steep curve and up the other side. With a powerful lift, she went into a 540-degree spin and landed perfectly.

Mel switched into some grinds on the coping followed by some "big airs."

Only 25 seconds left. Fired up by the crowd, Mel decided to finish with a trick she had been working on for weeks – it was called a brainless.

As Mel launched into a backflip and began to spin, time seemed to stop, like a video on freeze-frame. For one terrifying moment, she was out of control and falling. The crowd gasped as she landed off balance – and just managed to stay on her feet. But would that scrappy landing lose her points?

"Mel! Gimme five!" The other skaters crowded round. Mel had scored just high enough to qualify.

"That was a great run! You were really catching air," said Mel's friends. "What a cool truespin kindgrind! And where did that brainless come from?"

Mel looked up and grinned as she unbuckled her skates. It was the usual skate talk – but now they were talking about her, and she loved it! ❖

Steep skiing

It was perfect skiing weather. The sun was shining, and knee-deep powder snow had fallen during the night.

On days like these, steep skiers long for a magic carpet to whisk them up the mountain so they can ski steep, deserted slopes of pure new snow.

Today, Jason and some of the world's most daring skiers were doing just that. They were competing in the World Extreme Skiing Championships in Valdez, Alaska. There were no ski resorts in this remote place – just endless snow-covered valleys and towering peaks.

Instead of a magic carpet, the competitors had a helicopter to take them to the top of Double Edge Mountain. Crouching beneath the whirling rotors, the skiers climbed on board for their first run of the day.

Skiing down Everest
One of the world's most daring skiers, Davo Karnicar from Slovenia, skied down Mount Everest after climbing to the top.

The helicopter whipped up a small blizzard of soft snow as it landed, and Jason and the other skiers climbed out. After the skiers had waved the helicopter off, the only sounds were the wind and the crunching of footsteps.

On the mountaintop, the competitors were more like friends than rivals. Few people got to see sights like these.

"Nearly perfect snow, Jason," said one. "No risk of an avalanche."

"Well, I've got my beacon," said Jason, patting his pocket. "And you better dig like crazy if I have to use it!"

Avalanches

Avalanches are deadly snow-slides high up in the mountains. If a skier is buried, his beacon sends a signal to rescuers.

Avalanches are not the only hazard extreme skiers face. They also risk broken bones as they head down slopes as sheer as the side of a skyscraper.

Jason clicked into his bindings and looked down the course. It was a valley called the White Room – steep enough to turn a hobby skier snow-white with fear. After a three second countdown, Jason launched himself off the mountain.

Faster and faster he sped down the slope, leaving a twisting trail in the snow. Carving from side to side, he just managed to control his speed. His skis skipped on and off the snow as he leaped from turn to turn.

Jason plunged into a steep ice gully where several skiers had taken some nasty tumbles on the previous day.

Safely through the gully, Jason skied toward a cornice. The giant lip of snow on the edge of the cliff was the perfect launch pad for a "big air."

"Nothing in the world beats this," he thought as he took off like an eagle and dropped neatly onto the snow below.

From the top of the run, the competition base had been a distant speck. Now, the slope was leveling off, and Jason could hear a roar of applause as he neared the finish line.

The judges and crowd had followed his lightning run and dazzling jumps on a giant-screen TV. There was a bigger cheer when his score went up: 134 points made him the winner of the day!

"And tomorrow's run will be even better," thought Jason. ❖

FINISH

Freestyle motocross

Mike Marshall sat astride his dirt bike and gazed across the huge empty arena. He nodded with satisfaction. Two big yellow diggers had carved out an awesome freestyle motocross course at a Las Vegas stadium.

Freestyle motocross
Freestyle motocross riders launch their dirt bikes off earth mounds and wooden ramps to pull off amazing tricks. Their sport draws huge crowds in the U.S.

Mike scanned the small mountain range of earth ramps, humps, and bowls and planned his moves for the contest the next day. "I'll go for a lazy boy on the first ramp, and a bar hop over there."

Mike kick-started his bike and began to cruise the course. On a high ramp, he could not resist one stunt. Leaning across the handlebars, he gripped the front mudguard with both hands. A fender grab was not the most difficult trick to pull, but it drew whistles and applause from the small group of fans and mechanics watching from the stands.

On contest day, thousands of people packed the huge stadium. The arena rocked with music and cheering.

Mike buckled up his boots and pulled on his helmet. He bounced impatiently on the bike as he waited for his round.

"And now – MIKE MARSHALL!" blared the loudspeakers.

Mike had just two minutes to show what he could do. He revved the engine, raced up the first ramp, and jumped the bike high in the air. As he soared, Mike flipped the bike sideways and swung his leg over the saddle and brought it down on the other side of the bike. It was a perfect nac-nac.

Stunts and tricks

Many freestyle motocross riders pedal their way to success! They practice their stunts on BMX bikes before trying them out at high speed on a dirt bike.

Bikes for jumps
Freestyle motocross bikes
are light and powerful.
Extra-bouncy suspension
(springing) softens the
impact of landing.

At each ramp, Mike pulled off
another daring stunt. The crowd was
just a blur, but he could sense that
people were on the edge of their seats.

"I could win this!" thought Mike.

Just one more insane trick to go.
Twisting the throttle right back, Mike
tore up the ramp.
He was flying as
high as a house
when he leaped up
from the bike and
gave a cocky wave
to the crowd.

That wave was Mike's big mistake.
He took his eyes off the bike for just an
instant, but when he looked back the
bike was spinning away from him.
Mike made a desperate grab for the
seat, but he was too late. The bike
landed with a sickening crunch at the
bottom of the ramp, and Mike was
thrown head over heels into the dirt.

There was silence as two paramedics rushed to check him over.

"I'm fine. I'm okay," said Mike, as they helped him to his feet.

"So what do you call that jump?" asked one of the paramedics.

"Loser's leap," said Mike, "because I'm sure it just lost me a medal." ❖

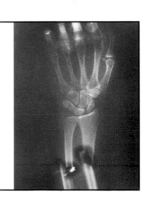

X for eXtreme – or X-ray?
Jumping a bike high takes nerve, but landing safely requires skill. Some riders learn this the hard way by breaking a leg or – as this X-ray shows – two bones in an arm.

BASE jumping

"Don't do anything dangerous!" shouted the truck driver. The three base jumpers clambered out at the foot of Four Horseman – a 1,300-foot high cliff close to the Colorado River.

Danger was just what Jessica, Liz, and Ross had in mind. Today, a strong wind was making jumps risky. But they planned to camp overnight and leap off the cliff at dawn when the air would be calm.

Corcovado base jump
A base jumper scaled a 120-foot high statue of Christ on Corcovado Mountain in Brazil to jump from the hand.

For Jessica, this trip was extra special. She had already jumped from three of the four objects that gave the sport its name – B for a building, A for an antenna, S for a span, or bridge. Four Horseman would be her E for earth. Then she would be part of the world's most unusual and risky sports club.

B
for building

A
for antenna

S
for span or bridge

E
for earth

The three friends pitched their tent below the cliff, ate a quick meal, and crawled into their sleeping bags.

"Bleep. BLEEEEEP!" The alarm woke Jessica first. "It's half past five — we should be at the exit point in an hour," she said, shaking her friends awake.

The little group followed the steep path to the cliff's top. Some early-bird jumpers were already disappearing over the edge of the cliff.

Jessica felt excited and terrified as she waited her turn. "You go first," said Liz, gently nudging her forward.

Base jumping in Moab
The huge cliffs around Moab, Utah, on barren land with few roads, are one of the few legal sites for U.S. base jumpers.

Jessica checked her gear and took her first peek at the dizzy drop beneath her. "3-2-1-see-ya!" she shouted. Taking a deep breath, she spread her arms and

plunged from the cliff. For two seconds Jessica plummeted like a stone before releasing her pilot chute. Above her the parachute surged open with a snap and filled with air, stopping her fall with a jerk. Now Jessica was swooping over the sandy plain like a bird.

Expertly pulling the steering toggles, she turned the parachute toward the sun. Then a tug on the toggles lifted her over a rocky ridge. But a gust of wind caught the chute, spinning her toward the cliff.

Base-jumping gear

Jumpers throw out a small pilot chute, which inflates and pulls open the main parachute. Chutes have to be checked and packed very carefully.

Jessica missed the cliff face by just a few feet, but now she was coming in to land too fast. She aimed for the river.

"Even if I land badly the water will break my fall," she thought as she hit the surface in a cloud of spray.

All around her, brilliantly colored parachutes floated to the ground. Then she saw Ross watching her from dry land.

"Brilliant, Jess! Are you up for another jump?"

"Not for me," laughed Jessica. "I've done E for earth now – and W for wet!" ❖

Want to see more?

Extreme sports are becoming more and more popular. Extreme versions of the Olympics, such as the X Games and The Gravity Games, draw huge crowds in cities around the world. Millions more watch the sports on TV.

The oldest street sport, skateboarding, is among the most exciting.

Speed climbers compete against the clock – and each other.

Inline street skaters perform on ramps and rails.

TV cameras track sky surfers as they board in thin air.

Wakeboarders use skate- and snowboard skills on water.

Street luge fans go downhill fast lying on adapted skateboards.

BMX tricks take two-wheeled daring to the limit.

Events include speed climbing, skateboarding, wakeboarding, sky surfing, street luge, motocross, inline skating, and BMX.

These contests are places where fans can check out the latest music, videos, clothes, and equipment – and share some of the thrill of living life close to the edge.

Freestyle is just one of several kinds of extreme motocross.

Glossary

Antenna
A metal mast that sends out or receives radio waves.

Beacon
A safety radio that is used by skiers in trouble to signal their position.

Binding
A clip that locks a skier's boot tightly onto the ski.

Blizzard
A snowstorm whipped up by a powerful wind.

BMX
Bicycle motocross involves stunt riding over obstacles.

Coping
A metal bar fixed along the top of a skating ramp.

Everest
The world's highest mountain, in Nepal and China; Everest is 29,050 feet high.

Final
The last stage in a contest that decides the winner.

Gully
A deep trench on a mountainside.

High-flotation jacket
An air-filled jacket that helps to keep the wearer afloat.

Paramedic
A medical worker who treats injuries and tends injured people until they get to a hospital.

Raft
An inflatable boat used for whitewater rafting.

Rapids
A narrow or shallow section of river where water flows very fast.

Revving
Increasing the speed of an engine.

Steep skiing
Skiing down very steep slopes or in risky places.

Steward
An official who makes sure that a competition is run safely and according to the rules.

Throttle
A control on a motorcycle that adjusts the speed of the engine.

Toggles
Loops that can be used to steer a parachute.

Trials
The early stages of a competition that decide who will go on to compete in the final.

Vert ramp
A U-shaped ramp with walls that become vertical near the top.

Whitewater
Stretches of fast-flowing river that bubble with white foam.

X-ray
An invisible beam of energy that can pass through solid objects; X-ray photographs show the bones inside the body.

Index

Real extreme sports enthusiasts pictured in our stories: international rafting teams from the Camel Whitewater Challenge; inline skater, Brigitte Ciardelli; competitors in the World Extreme Skiing Championships; freestyle motocross rider, Dave Turner; base jumpers, Lisa Barton and Mick Knutson.